BOBOGYI
A Burmese Spiritual Figure

BOBOGYI
A Burmese Spiritual Figure

Bénédicte Brac de la Perrière
Cristophe Munier-Gaillard

Preface by
Donald M. Stadtner

RIVER
BOOKS

First published in 2019 by River Books Co., Ltd
396 Maharaj Road, Tatien, Bangkok 10200 Thailand
Tel: (66) 2 225-4963, 2 225-0139, 2 622-1900
Email: order@riverbooksbk.com
www.riverbooksbk.com

Publisher: Narisa Chakrabongse
Production Supervisor: Paisarn Piemmettawat
Design: Ruetairat Nanta

ISBN: 978 616 451 027 2

Cover: Golden Valley's Bobogyi, Yangon. © Cristophe Munier-Gaillard
Inside title page: Kyaikkhauk Pagoda Bobogyi in Thanlyin, pointing the location of
the Shwedagon Pagoda in Yangon. © Cristophe Munier-Gaillard
Opening pages: Mandalay Bobogyi, detail of his right hand with rings of
semi-precious stones given by devotees. © Cristophe Munier-Gaillard
Back cover: Devotees of Golden Valley's Bobogyi meeting at the altar.
© Cristophe Munier-Gaillard

Printed and bound in Thailand by Bangkok Printing Co., Ltd.

Contents

PREFACE

Few going to Burma, or Myanmar, have not visited the Shwedagon Pagoda but few realize that this premier national monument owes its very existence to a reformed ogre residing in central Yangon at Sule Pagoda. His name today is Sule pagoda Bobogyi and his role in Burma's history goes back all the way to the time of the Enlightenment at Bodh Gaya when the Buddha presented hair relics to two brothers hailing from Yangon. These very hair relics are now believed to be enshrined in the Shwedagon.

The Buddha prophesied that the brothers would return home and enshrine the holy strands inside a *stupa*, together with other relics left by other Buddhas who visited Yangon and converted ogres. The brothers returned to Yangon and, with the local king and the god Thagya Min, located the other relics on Shwedagon Hill; these were then enshrined in a *stupa*, with the hair relics, in what became the Shwedagon Pagoda, according to *The Glass Palace Chronicle*, or *Hmannan Mahayazawindawgyi*, a national chronicle compiled in the second quarter of the nineteenth century. But local Mon and Burmese chronicles tell a different story, claiming that the whereabouts of the relics were forgotten and lost since many eons had elapsed since the Buddhas visited Yangon.

Thagya Min then enlisted the help of the local ogres who had been converted by the previous Buddhas, an episode known from a Mon chronicle, *Slapat Rajawan Datow Smin Ron*, dated to 1766. All the ogres then helped locate the relics on Shwedagon Hill. Two of the ogres were associated with trees, the Acacia and the Bael, and others with specific locations in Yangon and in nearby Hmawbi. These locations probably represented real shrines at the time, each of which enhanced its fame by linking their histories to the overarching myth of the Shwedagon. The Shwedagon did not spawn these related sites but rather the lesser sites deliberately attached their narratives to far more sacred *stupa* or temples. This phenomena of lesser sites piggybacking on more popular sacred sites is witnessed throughout the Theravada world.

The myths enveloping the Shwedagon changed however after the British took Yangon in the 1850s and designated the Sule pagoda as the hub of the new city. Memory of the other ogres soon faded, hastened by this meteoric rise of the Sule pagoda at the city's center. In this way Sule Bobogyi rose to prominence alone in his role in the Shwedagon myth.

Sule Bobogyi directed the brothers, the local king and Thagya Min to Shwedagon Hill by pointing north, in the direction of the Shwedagon, with his outstretched right arm. This dramatic moment in the Shwedagon story comes to life for devotees who worship a life-size wooden image of Bobogyi whose raised right arm points in the direction of the Shwedagon. Just such a figure appears in a rare early twentieth-century photograph (see page 23). The steps by which the converted ogre Sule Bobogyi became woven into the Shwedagon myth, his ties to beliefs in Bobogyi figures more generally, and the role of Bobogyi figures today in Burma has been unraveled brilliantly by Bénédicte Brac de la Perrière, a foremost authority on *nats*, or 'spirits', in Burma.

This Sule Bobogyi, standing with his outstretched right arm, has now been copied at numerous *stupa* sites. These figures, placed in separate shrines on pagoda platforms, point in the direction of the central stupa; but the narratives, or myths, associated with these sites do not include the feature of lost relics. There is therefore no need for images to be shown pointing, apart from directing worshippers attention to the central *stupa*. For example, large pointing Bobogyi images appear at the Mahamuni Temple, Mandalay, and the Botataung *stupa*, Yangon.

Similar figures shown pointing with an outstretched right arm include several key Buddha images who are shown prophesying the rise of cities, usually from nearby hilltops. The best-known example is the standing Buddha on Mandalay Hill, pointing south to the future site of the Mandalay Palace. This was created by Mindon (r. 1853-1878). Another, across the Irrawaddy from Pagan, is a huge wooden Buddha pointing across the river to the future capital. A further example is on a hilltop across the Irrawaddy from the famous Sri Ksetra. Apart from the example in Mandalay, it is hard to fix a date to this tradition of 'pointing' Buddha figures, but the image of Bobogyi at the Sule may have connections with the tradition of pointing Buddhas, perhaps arising sometime in the second half of the nineteenth century, if not much earlier. 'Pointing Buddhas' may now and then appear in other Theravada societies but this special type of imagery can be strongly associated with Burma, much like the 'Walking Buddha' that is so characteristic of Thailand.

The day to day worship of Bobogyi in Golden Valley, a Yangon neighborhood, is chronicled in Part II by Cristophe Munier-Gaillard, an indefatigable researcher who has devoted many years to understanding later Burmese mural art. His numerous photographs, taken over a period of many months, capture the flavor of local worship and the diverse modes of devotion.

These two thoughtful essays explore the complex interactions between so-called indigenous faiths and Pali Buddhism. The local legends surrounding Sule Bobogyi and the steps by which this deity entered into national Buddhist legends, illustrates not only the elastic nature of myths but also how sacred narratives are forever evolving in unforeseen directions.

Donald M. Stadtner
Walnut Creek, California

PART I

Ceremonial hall with the Thirty-seven Lords in front of Thamaing Bobogyi's altar, Yangon.

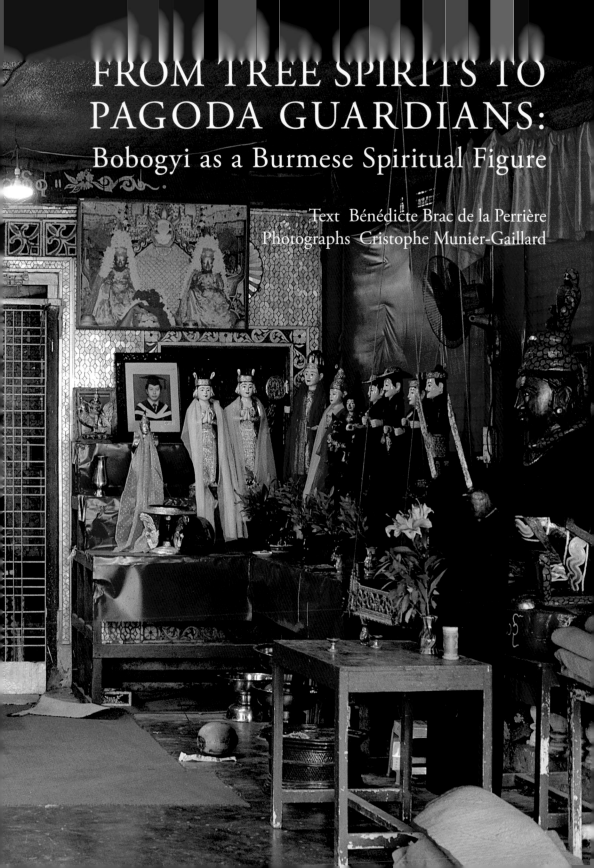

FROM TREE SPIRITS TO PAGODA GUARDIANS:
Bobogyi as a Burmese Spiritual Figure

Text Bénédicte Brac de la Perrière
Photographs Cristophe Munier-Gaillard

At the corner of lanes, hanging on majestic trees or duly hosted on the platform of well-known pagodas, the pervasive and comforting presence of *bobogyi*[1] may be felt everywhere in Burma, all the more so because their images have grown in number, in size and in magnificence in their multiple contemporary settings. *Bobogyi* are standing old men clinging to their stick, usually dressed in white like religiously inclined people and with their head topped by a divine ornament. They all look similar as if they were reflections of a single ubiquitous appearance emerging from an undifferentiated narrative. But they are only protective beings, the collective product of the locals' care, with an often unrecognized identity merely determined by the place where they have taken shape, such as Thamaing Bobogyi in Yangon[2] or Shwe Nyaung Bin Bobogyi along the road to Pegu (**1, 2**).[3] These places have become in the course of time fully developed sanctuaries of a more or less local importance, identified by signboards with a diverse terminology (**3-5**). Such is the story of Cristophe Munier-Gaillard's dedicated observation and documentation of the daily life of Golden Valley's Bobogyi, whose shrine happens to have ossified in a well-to-do neighborhood of Yangon. The second part of this book consists of this pictorial narrative of the furtive day-

1. New car 'prostrating itself' three times in front of Shwe Nyaung Bin Bobogyi shrine: the car moves to the front and then to the back, three times, while being blessed by the head of the Bobogyi shrine. Note the offering basket on the roof presented to Bobogyi, which will then be placed inside the sanctuary.

2. Owner of a vehicle making an offering to Shwe Nyaung Bin Bobogyi (pink scarf).

3. Mandalay Bobogyi *biman*. Entrance of the sanctuary of Mandalay Bobogyi, Mandalay Hill.

4. *Thathana pyu* Thamaing Bobogyi *nat nan*. Entrance of the sanctuary of Thamaing Bobogyi, Yangon.

5. Thingangyon Bobogyi *nat kun*. Former signboard of the sanctuary of Thingangyon Bobogyi, Yangon.

6. Myinbyushin Bobogyi. Entrance of Myinbyushin Bobogyi's temple at Taungbyon near Mandalay.

to-day gestures of passers-by, which reveals the benevolent figure of Golden Valley's Bobogyi emerging out of these urban encounters. In this first part, I address the emergence of *bobogyi* as a specific spiritual figure in the Burmese cosmology starting from the perspective of its outstanding place in the making up of Yangon contemporary city imaginary.

Bobogyi is both a generic term and a term of address which denotes great age and the respect that goes along with it. Translated as "respected grandfather" by Mandy Sadan,[4] it bespeaks of the attitude of deference that this figure deserves. The term is used to designate and address all sorts of beings who pop out at noticeable places: the outskirts of villages, notable trees, landmarks, or primary Buddhist sanctuaries. To add to the pervasiveness of the figure, "Bobogyi" is used by devotees to address some of the Thirty-seven Lords (*nat*) who belong to the spirit possession pantheon inherited from the royal worship of tutelary spirits.[5] This is the case of Alon Bobogyi or Myinbyushin (**6**)

Signboards identifying shrines of *bobogyi* display a varied terminology which changes according to the status of the place. *Biman* that qualifies Mandalay Bobogyi temple evokes its institutionalized status at Mandalay foothill. The entanglement of the Thamaing Bobogyi worship within the spirit possession context, in Yangon, is indicated by the word *nat nan* "nat palace", the usual designation of spirit shrines, but it is also mitigated by the expression *thathana pyu* "taking care of the (Buddhist) religion". As for Thingangyon Bobogyi, his ubiquitous nature as a communal spirit is revealed by the term *nat kun*, "nat shrine" related to him. In Taungbyon, a village north of Mandalay dedicated to the worship of *nat*, no further information than his name is needed to locate the temple of Minbyushin, one of the members of the Thirty-seven Lords pantheon.

7. *Yokkaso*, the tree guardian. After R. C. Temple 1906.

or even such popular male figures as U Min Kyaw and U Min Lay when addressed by particularly reverential worshippers.[6]

As a tree spirit, *bobogyi* seems related to *yokkaso*, a term of Pali origin that identifies a kind of being in Burmese erudite cosmological discourses. In Reginald Temple's gorgeous illustrations of the Burmese spiritual world, he has been pictured as an ethereal being (**7**) appearing out of thick tree foliage.[7] In rural contexts, *yokkaso* and *bobogyi* also share the ritual role of "communal spirit" as documented by Melford Spiro who describes – for Central Burma – a continuum

8, 9. *Yokkaso* of the banyan tree at the Shwe Nyaung Bin Bobogyi sanctuary, north of Yangon.

10-12. Sanctuary of Yangon Bobogyi under a huge banyan tree, at the southwest foothill corner of the Shwedagon pagoda, Yangon. Contrary to the Shwedagon Bobogyi located on the *stupa* platform, and in charge of the Buddhist relics (20), the Yangon Bobogyi is a communal spirit to whom members of the local community pay respect at each event of their life cycle (birth, initiation, marriage).

from the quick-tempered nature spirit (*yokkaso*) to the tutelary spirit addressed by the honorific term "Bobogyi".[8] In the contemporary urban context, *yokkaso*, who are known to induce visions of themselves in people they intend to interact with, share most features of their imagined appearance with urban trees' *bobogyi* as if the latter were solidified instantiations of the former (**8, 9**). Particularly known in this function of communal spirits are Mandalay Bobogyi (**opening pages**) and Yangon Bobogyi (**10-12**).

13, 14. Tiny shelves with a *bobogyi* in Thingangyun and Golden Valley, Yangon (13: Brac de la Perrière, 2015).

The growing presence of *bobogyi* in the urban context

In the eighties, when I began to roam throughout Yangon in a quest to understand the city's spiritual life, the *bobogyi* spirits were usually made manifest on mere shelves hanging on the biggest trees: some incense sticks, a glass of water, a candle or a pot with rose-apple leaves were enough to signal the presence of a spirit. If there was any representation at all, then it was most often limited to a small rustic wooden figurine. We must recall that for many people in Burma, the time was then one of restriction and privation, even in well-to-do neighborhoods. At the head of the state party, Ne Win had imposed his *Burmese Way to Socialism* and closed the country to foreign influences and business. Goods and commodities were kept out of reach, movement and travel were strictly controlled and lives were limited to vital needs. Things changed somewhat after the second coup, in 1988, when a new junta started to open the country to a market economy. With more opportunities to grow richer, at least for some people, *bobogyi*'s popularity increased, as apparent from the rise in number and size of their figured representations. The new era allowed *bobogyi* to acquire a more substancial existence. Standard painted statues resembling R.C. Temple's angel-like picture with its divine headdress (**7**) mushroomed on the shelves (**13, 14**) and got taller (**15-18**). With time, the shelves could not accomodate the images anymore. Wooden niches on stilts were soon erected under the trees in which more diversified offerings could be presented to the spirit. Finally, permanent structures were placed at the main *bobogyi* spots, particularly during the wave of repairs that followed the devastating Nargis cyclone in 2008, which damaged so many notable trees in the city.

15, 16. *Bobogyi* at the Tamway main crossroad, Yangon.

17, 18. Another *bobogyi* a hundred meters from the Tamway main crossroad, Yangon.

Shrines, such as that of Golden Valley's Bobogyi, became a common feature of the urban landscape constructed to protect larger and larger statues. These are most often well-tended, regularly refurbished and richly presented with offerings. All of a sudden, spirits inhabiting the trees in the Burmese imaginary (*yokkaso*) had been displaced by more and more solidified and standardized forms known as *bobogyi*. A process of materialization had given shape to them in the urban context and allowed for new forms of devotion.

Bobogyi as pagoda guardians

19. Yayle Bobogyi, Kyauktan.

Significantly, these tree *bobogyi* also resemble their corresponding figures in a number of pagodas. Indeed, the contemporary iconographic material of Buddhist sanctuaries often comprises newly manufactured images of old men holding a walking stick (**19, 20**) often dressed in white or in light colors.

They commonly appear in a surrounding of *weikza* figures, a class of beings whose religious virtuosity and esoteric knowledge is supposed to go with a range of powers claimed today by numerous devotees.[9] Like the tree *bobogyi* statues, pagoda *bobogyi* and *weikza* – both belonging to contemporary Buddhist iconographic material – are crafted wooden statues of considerable size whose painted finish is regularly refreshed. This iconographic material may easily be identified as pertaining to a new era of affluence, which began with the opening to market economy in the nineties, or to what I would like to call the "SLORC style", developed in the wave of Buddhist monument refurbishing undertaken under the aegis of the junta. Figures of *bobogyi* and *weikza*,

20. Shwedagon Bobogyi and the walking sticks offered to him in gratitude. Shwedagon pagoda, Yangon.

newly settled on pagoda platforms in considerable numbers, share characteristics of longevity, wisdom and benevolence that make them fit into the Buddhist sanctuary setting. However, as perceptively stated by Mandy Sadan,[10] they also differ in one important point: in that a pagoda *bobogyi* is linked to its location and cannot be propitiated elsewhere through portable representations or various presencing practices, as is the case of the *weikza*.

While Sadan interprets this "earthbound territoriality" as the mark of pagoda *bobogyi*'s closeness to lower spirits such as the Thirty-seven Lords,[11] I would like to nuance this stance by emphasizing another particularity of those figures: their role as actual pagoda guardians. Other characteristics of *bobogyi* figures could also be highlighted, such as their usual abstinence from taking over the bodies of devotees through spirit possession. This avoidance could actually allow one to understand them as being better located than lower spirits on the Burmese spiritual scale of values. To explain why would require us to dig into complex and obscure ritual histories. However, what should be highlighted is the deeply ingrained perception of pagoda *bobogyi* as guardians of religion. Indeed, they are represented as instrumental agents of local Buddhicization narratives. This role of the *bobogyi* ranks him on a par with the *weikza*, who also stand as caretakers of Buddha's teachings, although the *bobogyi*'s mandate is concerned with the local protection of Buddhism rather than with the broader one.

Bobogyi in the legend of the Shwedagon pagoda

In Yangon, especially, a specific *bobogyi* narrative has developed that came to inform the standard figure over time. This narrative is part of the foundation legend of the Shwedagon pagoda, the prestigious Buddhist *stupa* whose golden spire still illuminates the city skyline (**22**). It is only in 1757 that Alaungpaya, king of Ava, founded Yangon around the Shwedagon pagoda because of the good port facilities of the site. It was then chosen by the British to establish their new colonized province in the 1850s and became the capital of Independent Burma in 1948, until 2004.[12] Besides Yangon's

21. Walking sticks to be offered to Kyaikkhauk pagoda Bobogyi, Thanlyin. The sticks correspond to the good health and long life granted by Bobogyi.

22. Shwedagon pagoda, Yangon. (RB)

good port facilities, the presence of the famous *stupa* definitely marked the site as an ancient Buddhicized place fit to become the new capital of Burma. After independence in 1948, in the urge to reassert the new nation as Buddhist entity, various shrines of Yangon came to be linked to the Shwedagon narrative which became a nation-defining myth (**23**).

Nothing more than the legend of the Shwedagon pagoda could better exemplify the role of *bobogyi* as agents of local Buddhicization in the contemporary Burmese imaginary. This legend deals with pagoda hair relics received by natives of Lower Burma from the Buddha's hands. It has been the fertile ground on which the successive developments of the city imaginary have spring up, particularly around the figure of King Okkalapa – a legendary king of the Dannawadi kingdom, that is, old Thwante, about ten miles across the river from Yangon. Other important traditions for Lower Burma pagodas stem from fifteen-century myths about the Buddha granting six hair relics to six hermits that rather involve the Suvanabhumi kingdom –Thaton, north Tenasserim. Both narratives concur to make the gift of hair relics the main theme of Lower Burma Buddhicization legends to which the figure of *bobogyi* will later become essential.

The basic theme concerning the gift of the hair relics is found in Buddhist Pali sources. The earliest statement linking this episode to the Shwedagon pagoda are the three fifteen-century lithic inscriptions that can still be seen today on the east side of the Shwedagon hill and were installed

when King Dhammaceti was ruling in Pegu (AD.1472-1492).[13] According to this record, when in Bodhgaya, Gotama Buddha gave eight hairs plucked from his head to two traveling merchant brothers, Tapussa and Bhallika, who were heading back to their country and needed something with which to worship him back home. The Dhammaceti inscription further relates that after some incidents, the brothers brought back and enshrined the relics on the hillock where the Shwedagon would be erected. However, the current main narrative that, in time, emerged from this scheme has it that King Okkalapa came with his army to welcome Tapussa and Bhallika on the spot where their boat landed. Then, the brothers presented the king with the relics and the king started to search for a place where he could enshrine them so that his people could worship them there.

The search for the right place to enshrine Buddhist relics is a common trope of many pagoda founding stories and a privilege of Buddhist kings. The right place is necessarily one that has already received a Buddhist dispensation as attested by *in situ* relics or by Buddha's prophecies. In this sense, this place is predestined and has to be disclosed through a new localization of Buddhism. This makes each founding story of a pagoda a tale of Buddhicization.

In the Shwedagon narrative, as recorded in a late Mon chronicle,[14] the brothers had been instructed by the Buddha in India to enshrine his hair relics where the three Buddhas who had visited Yangon in previous eras – Kakusandha, Konagamana and Kassapa – had left their own relics. King Okkalapa looked for the place in vain and had to ask for Sakka's help. Because Sakka was ruling over the divinities' abode, he was in the position to convene a meeting of very old spirits that could have attended the enshrining of the previous relics. And thus, these very old spirits – who are given the Pali names of Yawhani, Dekkhina and Amyittha in the Mon chronicle – were able to show where the previous relics would be found and where the new ones should be installed.[15]

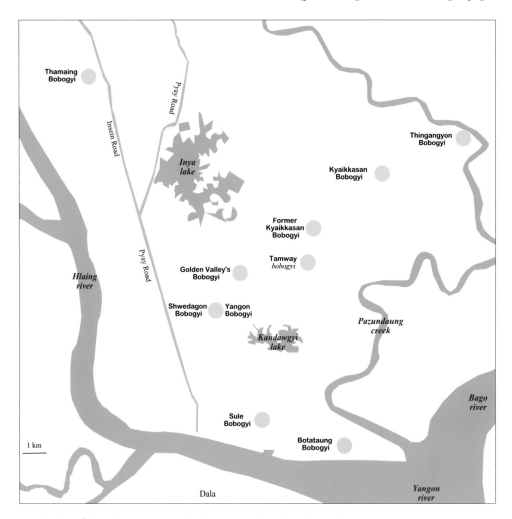

As the Shwedagon narrative is remembered today, the agents of the site discovery are very old spirits in charge of caring for the relics from the three previous Buddhist dispensations and awaiting their disclosure. These spirits are considered as formerly untamed spirits or ogres (*bilu*) who were pacified and turned into relic caretakers through their meeting with one of the three previous Buddhas. Indeed, the conversion of untamed place spirits, such as *bilu*, into pagoda guardians when they met a Buddha is a very pervasive theme of Buddhism localization across the Theravada world.

Thus, the Shwedagon story as set out by Dhammaceti and later chronicle writers bespeaks of a Buddhicization of the Irrawaddy delta dating back to the Buddha's lifetime. Other traditions refers to the concurrent narrative of the conversion of the king of Suvanabhumi (Thaton, north Tenasserim) by Gavampati, one of the Buddha's early followers who is supposed to have also given two Buddha hair relics to incorporate into two *stupa* to be built around Yangon (Kyaikkasan and Kyaikko). As a result, two distinctive traditions about the localization of Buddhism in the region exist, one from Thwante (Okkalapa narrative), the other one from Thaton, both involving the supposed transmission of hair relics by the living Buddha.

A third story, also referred to in the Shwedagon Dhammaceti's inscription, tells about the sending by the Indian Mauryan King Asoka of two missionaries, Sona and Uttara, to spread the Buddha's teaching in the same region, involving a second Buddhicization two centuries later. The Shwedagon *stupa*, then lost in brush and vegetation, is then supposed to have been rediscovered by the two missionary monks as a Buddhist site containing relics from the four successive Buddhas. Later on, various kings sought to extend their dominions to the delta through unsuccessful attempts to take the Shwedagon relics, such as the mythical king Duttabaung, King of Prome and Anawratha, King of Pagan (11th century). Instead, these kings had the *stupa* refurbished. Buddhist relics are attached to the site where they have been installed as a gesture of Buddhist localization and to remove them is considered a sacrilege.

Today, according to the shared Burmese imagination and as expounded in pagoda histories dating back to the fifties,[16] the four or five spirits who met under the aegis of Sakka on the eve of the foundation of the Shwedagon pagoda are envisioned as *bobogyi* who had already converted into their Buddhist existence. They are four in number, corresponding to the three previous dispensations plus the current one, or five in versions including the dispensation of the Buddha to come, Metteyya. They had already been converted on the occasion of previous Buddhas' visits to the region and had received relics to guard from them. At the founding meeting, Sakka is supposed to have also granted them the guardianship of ancient pagodas that stand in the visible vicinity of the Shwedagon pagoda, or where various episodes of the Shwedagon story took place: Sule, Botataung, Thanlyin (or Thingangyon, according to some versions) and Hmawbi. It may be said that, at various stages of Yangon urban expansion and due to the importance of the Shwedagon pagoda as a Buddhist sanctuary dominating the city landscape, the basic founding narrative of Buddhicization has been enhanced so as to include a number of neighboring ancient pagodas in one shared network, through *bobogyi* characters.[17]

24. Sule Bobogyi. Photograph, ca. 1905. After Walter del Mar 1906.

Sule Bobogyi

The meeting of the spirits was convened by Sakka, the ultimate defender of the teachings that compose Buddha's dispensation, at a place where the Sule pagoda was supposed to be erected and that served as the central point of the colonial Yangon city-grid planning. The oldest spirit who had been converted by the first Buddha having visited the place (Kakusandha) designated the site where the relics were concealed with his outstretched right arm. Today, a man-sized statue of an old man with his right hand stretched towards the Shwedagon stands in a pavilion at the northeast of the Sule platform. The figure is said to represent Sule Bobogyi showing the location to Sakka and King Okkalapa (**26**). Stadtner[18] states that Sule, an ancient Mon pagoda known for its single hair relic from Sri Lanka, was not linked with the Shwedagon narrative until the Second Anglo-Burmese war (1852-1853). Then elevated to the central point of the new colonial city, Sule soon became associated to the narrative of the rediscovery of the Shwedagon relics by the group of old spirits. A 1905 picture (**24**) of Sule Bobogyi with his entourage, King Okkalapa and the two merchant brothers, shows that it is likely to be the one standing *in situ* today.[19]

   The representation of Sule Bobogyi as a white-clad old man, clinging to a walking stick and pointing to the Shwedagon hill whose template may have originated in the image of the standing Buddha showing the spot of a new Buddhist city, occurring first in Mandalay,[20] may be said to be one of the oldest sculpted images of the *bobogyi* character. That image of a white-clad old man, clinging to a walking stick, has become

25. Amulets, statuettes and photos of Sule Bobogyi.

a model for pagoda guardians and tree spirits alike, all across Burma, while pointing to the site of the Shwedagon has spread only to a few sanctuaries around Yangon, i.e. the Thwante Bobogyi (**27**), Thanlyin Bobogyi (**inside title page**), Botataung Bobogyi (**29**) and Hmawbi *Bobogyi* (**35, 36**).

Since the mid-nineteenth century, the devotion to Sule Bobogyi has grown tremendously. In 1915, it was attended by a female medium,[21] but it is difficult to say what kind of ritual was dedicated to the *bobogyi* at this time. Today, the laymen in charge of the cult are not spirit mediums, but pious Buddhists employed by the pagoda body of caretakers. Devotees come to the *bobogyi* to ask him to grant wishes: students come to him to pass their exams, business men to be successful, and officials to be promoted to a better position. They make offerings consisting of a basin with a coconut, bananas, rose apple leaves, areca nuts and various paper decorations that are presented by the attendants in exchange for a bit of money. Basins are left in place for some time around the statue and removed by the attendants when the leaves have withered or when room is needed. The number of offerings and their magnificence are markers of the *bobogyi's* ever-growing fame among his devotees (**opening pages**). Rumors of the success he has granted in turn reinforce his attractiveness. Since the nineties, his pavilion has more often than not been stuffed with coconuts, all the more so because, being close to the city hall, he has gained in fame among high-ranking officials from the municipality. Some offerings made of golden coconuts have even been displayed for extended periods with ex-voto disclosing the identity of those among the *nomenklatura* officials who were benefiting from the *bobogyi's* protection. The impetus only slowed down after September 2007 when demonstrations of the monks against the government known as the Saffron Revolution created a crisis in the municipality administration. However, Sule Bobogyi has remained the most revered of the pagoda guardians and is widely known to be the discoverer of the Shwedagon relics.

27. Thwante Bobogyi, the new standing image pointing towards Shwedagon pagoda's direction, settled on the Shwesandaw pagoda in 2011, Thwante.

26. Sule Bobogyi, Sule pagoda, Yangon.

28. Thwante Bobogyi, Shwesandaw pagoda. Next to the new image, the old, small one is kept in a glass case. The old image is not pointing his index finger and is locally identified as a *yokkaso*. The juxtaposition of the old image and the new tall one nicely illustrate the contiguity of the *yokkaso* and *bobogyi* spiritual figures. The Shwesandaw pagoda is an ancient one containing a hair relic and is locally known to be part of the Shwedagon pagoda network.

29. A Thai devotee praying to **Botataung** Bobogyi whose finger is touching her forehead, while another devotee is wrapping him with a scarf.

30. Hung on the gong which is hit by the devotees, is an article from a Thai magazine on amulets about the power of Botataung Bobogyi, called the "angel who grants wishes".

Botataung Bobogyi

Botataung, where king Okkalapa is supposed to have welcomed the boat loaded with the Buddha hair relics, also has a *bobogyi* image linked to the narrative of the Shwedagon relics' discovery. According to Stadtner, it was only after Independence (1948) that the Botataung pagoda became associated with the reception of the hair relics by King Okkalapa.[22] Botataung was previously known to be an ancient hair relic pagoda without any particular link with the Shwedagon founding legend. However, World War II bombings created a breach in the sanctuary masonry, which resulted in the discovery of a hair reliquary. After Independence, the reconstruction of the pagoda became a national cause and the decision to keep the core of the building hollow was made so as to exhibit the relic. It is supposedly at this time that the Botataung pagoda was included in the Shwedagon founding narrative, because of its status as the place where the boat landed, along with the new tale of King Okkalapa giving back one of the hair relics to Tapussa so as to enshrine it in a local *stupa*. Botataung Bobogyi made his apparence in the Shwedagon narrative at this time with the mentioning of his presence at the Sule meeting. He is now represented in the Botataung pagoda, as a white-clad old man stretching his right arm towards the Shwedagon (**29**).

Now that Botataung pagoda has become a tourist attraction, with Thai travellers particularly attracted by the place (**29, 30**) since about a decade, the newly-rebuilt market of commodified religious goods has opened a special corner well provided with Thai-style glass amulets containing a miniature of Botataung Bobogyi, making it a body-portative image of a *bobogyi*, something not seen before anywhere else in Burma (**33**).[23] More Burmese artefacts such as wooden representations of Botataung Bobogyi or other religious figures to place on shrines, and even T-shirts, are also available in the market (**31, 32**).

31-33. Market of Buddhist images in front of Botataung pagoda. Several stands with Thai language information are dedicated to Bobogyi, selling amulets, T-shirts and statuettes.

34. Oldest of the three Hmawbi Bobogyi (in the left on figure 35).

Thamaing Bobogyi

Not surprisingly, the emergence of other *bobogyi* in the urban context – mainly after World War II – has reflected the dominance of the Shwedagon foundation narrative in the city's imaginary landscape. The growth of the city has been made possible by envisioning it in a spiritual landscape infused with the *bobogyi* figure. In this context, the *bobogyi* figures oscillate from the pagoda-attached relic custodians to the urban community-linked spirit, but definitely diverging from traditional tutelary spirits in that they cannot harm people when not placated. Two cases will be examined below, showing that the resulting cultic frameworks may vary considerably, those of Thamaing Bobogyi and of Kyaikkasan Bobogyi.

Thamaing Bobogyi is hosted in a small private temple outside of a pagoda setting. It serves as a communal place of worship in the northwestern suburb of Thamaing, which emerged before World War II. I was told the history of the place in February 2007, in the midst of a land conflict with the abbot in charge of the surrounding lands with "religious" status, who threatened to appropriate the allegedly encroaching temple. Thamaing Bobogyi temple was then run

35. Hmawbi Bobogyi, Zambu Mara Aung Zedi Daw, Hmawbi, in 2012 (Brac de la Perrière).

by a spirit medium, U Hla Gyi, who has since died. The story had just been written down by a learned inhabitant of the vicinity, building on Nyun Wai's version of the Shwedagon pagoda history.[24] According to the local historian, his grandfather, a wealthy man from the surrounding area, had seen in a dream Hmawbi Bobogyi, the ogre that had been converted by the second of the previous Buddhas of this era (Konagamana) and that had been appointed caretaker of Hmawbi pagoda situated to the north of Yangon (**34-36**). In the dream, Hmawbi Bobogyi was standing in a place of

36. Hmawbi Bobogyi, Zambu Mara Aung Zedi Daw, Hmawbi, in 2018.

shelter, at Thamaing, where he had rested on his way to the Sule meeting convened by Sakka. In the actual spatial configuration of the temple, the *bobogyi*'s statue turns its back to the Shwedagon. He is looking towards the west, his left hand raised to shade his eyes from the sunset light. The wealthy man ordered an image matching his vision to be made, installed it in a small sanctuary (**37, 38**), and appointed a male spirit medium to take care of it.

Thamaing Bobogyi is thus a localized version of one of the Shwedagon site discoverers, Hmawbi Bobogyi, who has been appropriated by the locals in the wake of urban development so as to create a communal place of worship connected to the city's Buddhicization narrative through a *bobogyi* figure. U Hla Gyi, the spirit medium running the place in 2007, told me that when the shrine was founded, "village" communal lands were dedicated to it. At that time, the surrounding space had not yet been consecrated "religious lands" for the two nearby pagodas founded later on. In other words, the establishment of a *bobogyi* sanctuary was a true gesture of Buddhicization at a time when no other Buddhist institution was present.

Of course, this discourse of the spirit medium running the place was recounted to me in the context of the land conflict with the two adjoining pagodas and was meant to advocate an antecedent right for the *bobogyi* land, over that of "religious" lands, a right that was eventually recognized by the authorities. Once the two pagodas were founded – also following a dream had by two brothers – the result was that, together with the *bobogyi* shrine, they formed three independent institutions as supposedly evidenced by the presence of three banyans, three wells and three tanks that have since disappeared. U Hla Gyi was also able to identify the lineage of four mediums that had run the temple since

37, 38. Thamaing Bobogyi, Yangon, in 2015 and 2018 (37: Brac de la Perrière).

its creation and to recount the institutional evolution of the site, which was first sponsored by wealthy men of the local community, and then by collective contributions from the ward inhabitants.

Thamaing Bobogyi is reputed to ensure the wellbeing of the local community by preventing fire and thefts. However, this eventually caused the original statue to be stolen and vandalized by thieves in circumstances that were confirmed by a dream. As a result, the locals collectively sponsored a new image to restore the site to a place of worship. U Hla Gyi once told me that, on this occasion, the new statue was sent to Hmawbi, to reside in the presence of the *bobogyi* for seven days as a confirmation of its link to the Shwedagon narrative figure. However, there is no other formal expression of Thamaing Bobogyi's affiliation with Hmawbi Bobogyi except that the theme of his joining the Sule meeting is ritually performed through offerings made by the spirit medium on the 13th of the waxing Tabaung moon (March) when the *bobogyi* is imagined to rest at Thamaing on his way to the annual Shwedagon pagoda festival.

Finally, if Thamaing Bobogyi emerged as the product of a true gesture of Buddhicization in a local setting, it is also very distinctive among the group of *bobogyi* affiliated with the Shwedagon narrative, both because it has evolved independently of any local Buddhist institution and because it is enmeshed in a context of spirit mediumship. Today, the *bobogyi* image stands at the center of the concrete altar, surrounded by a collection of the Thirty-seven Lords statues belonging to U Hla Gyi. As the spirit medium explained to me, in spite of his scruples, the new *bobogyi* representation looks more like he is wiping sweat off his forehead with the back of his left hand rather than forming a shield over his eyebrows, probably because of a craftsman's error. It could be made right by turning back the hand from the elbow joint, U Hla Gyi wondered, but he dared not alter the figure. What he has done since taking over the shrine, in 1991, was to have the altar rebuilt and a ceremonial hall, to accomodate ceremonies to the Thirty-seven Lords, created and erected in front (**Part I opening pages**). Indeed, this move transformed the *bobogyi* sanctuary into a place hosting spirit possession at a time when getting a permit from the local authorities to perform such ceremonies in the streets – in front of the sponsor house as was formerly the case –, became a nuisance. That is how the Thamaing Bobogyi temple became the venue of spirit possession ceremonies for a whole network of spirit mediums connected to U Hla Gyi or who had settled in the surroundings, in addition to being a communal ritual place for the locals.

This evolution of the shrine in turn had consequences for the *bobogyi* ritual treatment. In particular, when he took over the temple, U Hla Gyi made a request to the *bobogyi* to take his representation once a year in procession around the ward before proceeding to the ritual shower, a task which he has duly performed until his death, thereby allowing the locals to celebrate their protective figure on this festive occasion. Thus, unlike other pagoda-resting *bobogyi* that as stated by Sadan, are not portable,[25] the Thamaing Bobogyi statue is taken on a procession every year as is done for the main statues of the Thirty-seven Lords to start their festival in their original place. However, unlike the tutelary spirits of the Thirty-seven Lords, Thamaing Bobogyi does not as a rule possess his spirit medium. According to U Hla Gyi, only on five occasions has the Thamaing Bobogyi taken over his body during the performance of spirit possession, and these occasions were to prevent fire and theft in the locality. On the occasion of the annual celebration in 2007, in the context of the land conflict pitting U Hla Gyi against the neighboring monk, Thamaing Bobogyi did manifest himself during the last series of possession dances closing the three-day event.

The *bobogyi* entered his medium, U Hla Gyi, looking very old and tired, and was asked by the audience about the prospects for the locality in the coming year, as well as worryingly questioned about what to expect as a settlement for the current land case. Then, once the final rituals had been performed, all of a sudden, U Hla Gyi's assistant called insistently for a tea pot and poured the burning liquid onto his head to the dread amazement of the public. Thus the *weikza* Bo Min Gaung, who was not supposed to interfere in a spirit possession ceremony, was inviting himself to the *bobogyi* abode due to the difficulties faced – at least that was the interpretation of the locals. Later on, once the case had been closed thanks to the intervention of local authorities, I was told that this manifestation of Bomingaung coming to the rescue of Thamaing Bobogyi impressed the local officials to such an extent that they decided to act in favor of the *bobogyi*.

The entanglement of the Thamaing Bobogyi cultic framework with a spirit mediumship context allows for occasional spirit possession by the *bobogyi*, although it differs from possession by other spirits. In this regard, the *bobogyi* emerges as very different from others, who are pagoda guardians or tree spirits, addressed by offerings made *in situ* and who do not indulge in entering their devotees through spirit possession dances. It seems that the Thamaing shrine autonomy as a communal/private ritual place has been harshly contested by the local Buddhist institutions. However, spirit mediums in charge of the place have managed to preserve this autonomy to their benefit through a strategy making good use of the locally-established link to the Shwedagon narrative through Hmawbi Bobogyi.

However, the linking of Thamaing Bobogyi to a spirit possession context, seemingly dragging him back to the lower status of spirits such as the Thirty-seven Lords, emerges as a specificity of a local context. Conversely, it could be said that for U Hla Gyi, being a dedicated servant of a *bobogyi* temple allowed him to reframe his spirit medium status so as to look more in tune with mainstream Buddhism. Indeed, he told me that, contrary to many spirit mediums, he did not fear to see his spirits flee when he went through ordination for a temporary stay at the monastery, which he did on a yearly basis. Indeed, he was authorized to do so by the *bobogyi* who, being a pagoda founder could not say 'no'. In fact, U Hla Gyi's connection with the pagoda guardian was part of a set of strategies designed by many urban spirit mediums today to cope with the new constraints imposed on their practice

by the authorities and to resist the criticisms of superstition from an increasingly prevalent mainstream Buddhism.[26] In this regard, the development of the *bobogyi* imaginary and devotion may rather correspond to a shift in spirit-possession configuration. Spirit mediums tend to turn to more Buddhist figures, like *bobogyi*, in order to cope with the more rigorous Buddhism of the urban environment.

39. Legend of the foundation of the Kaiykkasan pagoda. From left to right: pavilions of King Okkalapa, Sakka, and the hermit.

Kyaikkasan and Thingangyon Bobogyis

On the other side of Yangon, Kyaikkasan Bobogyi is another case of a *bobogyi* figure inspired by the Shwedagon founding legend. Kyaikkasan pagoda is an ancient *stupa* to the east of Shwedagon pagoda, in the middle of a vast stretch of land surrounded on three sides by a loop of the Ngamoyeik river and once tilled by Indian rice croppers. The built-up area around the pagoda expanded during the urban development that immediately followed Independence, until the whole extent of the land was incorporated into Yangon town administration in 1954, as Thingangyon municipality. In the wave of rewriting pagoda histories in the fifties, Kyaikkasan, which was known to have an ancient hair relic like the other pagodas belonging to the Shwedagon network, was reinvented as the recipient of a guardian *bobogyi* granted by Sakka during the Sule meeting, while at the same time it became the official pagoda (*zedi daw*) of the new municipality. However, well into the nineties, there was no *bobogyi* installed in the pagoda but only the hermit supposed to have taken part in the *stupa* foundation, Ba Khauk, who is represented as the figure of a brown-clad religious virtuoso linked to the second Buddhicization legend (**40-43**).[27] Two monumental ogres (*bilu*) also guarded the west gate of the monument (**44, 45**).

40. Statue of King Okkalapa and the mural relating his involvement in the founding of the Kyaikkasan pagoda. Kneeling in the middle, facing the pagoda, is the hermit.

41-43. Statue of the hermit Ba Khauk and the mural depicting his involvement in the founding of the Kyaikkasan pagoda; detail of his hat with the image of the pagoda.

However, a Kyaikkasan Bobogyi had long been well known and installed in a wooden niche under a huge banyan at the main road into the municipality. The small lead figurine (**47, 49**) had previously been donated to a nearby monastery then situated within the Insein municipality limits and was linked both to the Thirty-seven Lords and to an Indian deity: Mahapeinne (Ganesh). When the Thingangyon municipality was formed in 1954, the *bobogyi* let it be known that from now on he wanted to live on the Thingangyon main road. A spirit medium was ordered to find the site and to settle the new spirit abode (*nat sin*) for him. This is how the Kyaikkasan Bobogyi ended up outside of the pagoda, and became the communal guardian of the new municipality. Later on, after the second coup (1988), when the settlements extended well across the Ngamoyeik River in a new phase of urbanization, the Kyaikkasan Bobogyi had to move a third time. The construction of a national stadium had been decided together with a road-widening scheme for which the huge banyan had to be cut down. U Myin Aye, the engineer officer in charge of the public works, decided in 1993 to move the *bobogyi* to the other end of the municipality, just before the new bridge crossing over the river to serve the new satellite city, Dagon. U Myin Aye had also just settled in the new wealthy ward dedicated to high-ranking officials near the bridge. A small wooden shrine was erected on high piles (**47**) and a watcher living in the nearby deprived wards was appointed in return for small wages. The lead figurine was installed together with a new wood statue more resembling a standard *bobogyi*

44, 45. The two ogres (*bilu*) guarding the west gate of Kyaikkasan pagoda, Yangon.

(**47, 50**). Later on, in 2002, a rich entrepreneur made a donation of a third statue (**47, 51**).

In time, the shrine, situated on a major transportation axe for the new settlements, became a famous place of worship particularly for new car buyers converging there from the entire eastern section of Yangon to receive the blessings of the *bobogyi*. The shrine had also become the communal spirit of the adjoining ward, from which young boys entering the monastery or newlywed couples are presented to the *bobogyi* as if he were the 'village lord' (*ywadawshin*). Since 2002, a three-day spirit possession ceremony dedicated to the Thirty-seven Lords is organized every year by the community, under the supervision of the local elected chief in order to ensure the *bobogyi*'s protection, and for which a spirit medium is hired. However, the mediums are hardly possessed by *bobogyi*, only in a furtive way at the start of the day – a dreadful experience – because he is of a higher status than other spirits, being a custodian of Buddhist relics.

One can only highlight how different the story of Thamaing Bobogyi is from that of this communal shrine whose development has depended on local or less local official decisions with no spirit medium ever attached to it. Although the *bobogyi* existence is explicitly and iteratively related to the tale of the Kyaikkasan Bobogyi presence at the Sule meeting, today he is better known as Thingangyon Bobogyi, while the Kyaikkasan pagoda is now equipped with a full life-size standard statue of *bobogyi* (**46**) as well as representations of King Okkalapa receiving the relics surrounded by his entourage (**40**).

46. Kyaikkasan Bobogyi housed on the pagoda terrace.

47. Inside the sanctuary of
Thingangyon Bobogyi, Yangon.

Golden Valley's Bobogyi

The Golden Valley's Bobogyi is part of the group of urban,
community-linked spirits that have evolved seemingly
spontaneously from the day-to day devotion of local passers-
by. No connection to the founding legend of the Shwedagon
pagoda has ever been uncovered, though this *bobogyi* looks
exactly like standard pagoda treasure guardians. Dressed in
the usual white clothes, sometimes with slight variations due
to a fresh painting, the old man's aspect only varies according
to offerings of new scarves, flowers or religious artifacts.
Regular offerings include burning incense, lighting candles,
presenting betel leaves prepared for chewing or green leaves
in a vase, hanging jasmine garlands around his neck or
placing lit cigarettes in his hand. These many petty gestures
of care for the local spirit contribute to make its presence
felt in the neighborhood. More significant presentations are
flowers, food, offerings of bananas and coconuts attesting
to the intimate transactions between the devotees and the
Golden Valley's Bobogyi.

48. A group of *weikza* composed
of three representations of Bo Min
Gaung and two of Bo Bo Aung.
Sanctuary of Thingangyon Bobogyi,
Yangon.

One knows from the foundation plaque that the concrete
sanctuary was donated by a local family in 2005,
displacing the previous wooden shed that is now
used as a repository for discarded religious objects
that cannot be simply thrown away: a Chinese
shrine, a statue of Thuratati (Sarasvati), the Indian
goddess of knowledge, figurines of the Pegu Buffalo
medaw and her consort Athakuma. At the base of
the banyan all sorts of religious utensils are slowly
decaying: paper decorations, bamboo frames
and so on. Images of the Buddha, Shin Upagot,

U Ti Bwa, *weikza*, monks and spirits from the Thirty-seven pantheon, particularly Myinbyushin and U Min Kyaw, also stand as entourage to the *bobogyi*, picturing the whole Burmese religious world around him. The Golden Valley's Bobogyi emerges from this world to serve as a Buddhicized guardian, whose presence is continuously elaborated through the care of the local community.

49-51. From left to right: the earliest Thingangyon Bobogyi in lead, or Kyaikkasan Bobogyi, the second one held in a showcase (here without garlands), and the latest one (2002).

Bibliography

ANONYMOUS 1924, *Shwe Dagon Thamaing Athit* [The New History of Shwe Dagon], Rangoon.

ASARA (KYAIKKASAN) 1953, *Kyaikkasan cetitaw thamaing akyay* [Detailed history of Kyaikkasan zedi], Rangoon.

BRAC DE LA PERRIÈRE Bénédicte 1989, *Les rituels de possession en Birmanie. Du culte d'Etat aux cérémonies privées*. Paris, ADPF.

-------- 1995, « Urbanisation et légendes d'introduction du bouddhisme au Myanmar (Birmanie) », *Journal des Anthropologues*, no. 61-62, p. 41-66.

-------- 2011, « Being a Spirit Medium in Contemporary Burma », *Engaging the Spirit World. Popular Beliefs and Practices in Modern Southeast-Asia*, eds.

Kirsten W. Endres & Andrea Lauser, Asian Anthropologies 5, New York & Oxford: Berghahn Books, p. 163-184.

-------- 2014, « Spirits versus Weikza: Two Competing Ways of Mediation », in *Champions of Buddhism. Weikza Cults in Contemporary Burma*. Eds. Bénédicte Brac de la Perrière, Guillaume Rozenberg, and Alicia Turner, NUS Press Singapore : 54-79.

NYUN WAY 1989, *Htucha pyison thaw htamaing* [The Full and Extraordinary History], Rangoon.

PEARN B. R. 1939, *A History of Rangoon*, Rangoon: American Baptist Press.

PE MAUNG TIN 1934, « The Shwe Dagon Pagoda. » *The Journal of Burma Research Society*, 24.1, p. 1-91.

SADAN Mandy 2005, « Respected Grandfather, Bless this Nissan. Benevolent and Politically Neutral Bobogyi », *Burma at the turn of the 21st Century*, ed. by Monique Skidmore, Honolulu: University of Hawaii Press, p. 90-111.

SPIRO Melford 1967, *Burmese Supernaturalism: A Study in the Explanation and Reduction of Suffering*, Englewood Cliffs, NJ: Prentice-Hall.

STADTNER Donald M. 2011, *Sacred Sites of Burma. Myth and folklore in an Evolving Spiritual Realm*, Bangkok: River Books.

TEMPLE Reginald C. 1906, *The 37 Nats, a Phase of Spirit Worship Prevailing in Burma*. London: W. Criggs.

PART II

A YEAR IN THE LIFE
OF GOLDEN VALLEY'S
BOBOGYI

Text & photographs
Cristophe Munier-Gaillard

The Golden Valley's Bobogyi enjoys a privileged situation in the residential area that gives him his name. He is the guardian of a small banyan along the only road that runs through a labyrinth of alleys and dead-end lanes where few taxis dare to venture. This privileged situation explains the flow of daily offerings of which he is the recipient as early as the first streaks of dawn. I had been familiar with his altar for a long time and especially noticed the changes in clothing that Bobogyi's statue experienced. The colorful scarves he wore one day would disappear the next. He had a summer outfit but could also wear a thick orange linen jacket. Not to mention the fact that his face was repainted once a year. What a hectic life for a statue!

By accident my new address, in a nearby Yangon neighborhood, brought me into Bobogyi's presence. Otherwise, I would never have thought to contribute, even incidentally, to the knowledge of what his worship meant. But very quickly, indeed, my daily encounters inspired me with a sense of urgency: it was necessary to record the impermanence of this altar which crystallized the devotion of a whole quarter but also that of passers-by and street vendors, flower sellers, as well as collectors of scrap or glass. So I decided to keep a photographic journal of his metamorphoses and to visit him every day, first between 4:30 and 5:30 in the morning, then at noon and finally in the late afternoon. This documentation would one day surely become of interest to an anthropologist who could situate this worship in the perspective of Bobogyi's global cult.

The altar, occupying a small square meter at the side of the road, actually includes two worlds: a static and a dynamic one. The first, the world of the altar proper, at the foot of the banyan where the spirit of Bobogyi resides, includes the cult objects (vases, trays, bell, lighter, shelves, etc.) and a whole spiritual environment associated with the central statue of Bobogyi (statuettes of *nat*, deities, demiurge ascetics, the Buddha, photos of monks, etc.) that changes depending on the offerings. And then there is the court of the devotees. From the rich landowner to the deliverer of drinking water containers, a whole world gravitates around Bobogyi. I would discover later that their offerings made the banyan's inhabitants happy: this included the rats that lodged between its roots, and the squirrels that roamed along its bushy branches. They knew the time when, at dawn, one of the devotees came to offer, almost daily, about twenty brioches stuffed with cream. The squirrels were nibbling at those on the shelves of the altar, the rats at those around Bobogyi's feet. Nibbling on site but also to reserve food for future need: the rats came less to satiate themselves than to take their loot to their burrow. It also happened that dogs and crows wanted their share.

Although I never saw the ethereal Bobogyi dwelling in the banyan tree, but only his man-made statue, for me photographing Bobogyi and his altar resembled a spiritual practice. The shots were of two types. The ones where I was standing in the middle of the little intersection, photographing between two cars, always on the alert; and those where, with the eye on the viewfinder, I could immerse myself in the darkness of the camera for as long as I wanted. The viewfinder allowed me to isolate myself from the world and to see only Bobogyi. I experienced every shot as if a snorkeler, briefly surfacing for air but only to go back to a new detail, to another part of the altar. The viewfinder became the cloister where my mind no longer thought of or saw anything else. Suddenly, I felt a kind of exaltation during these sessions. In short, I could not have done most of these photographs without being in this state of aesthetic fervor. The devotees respected me with the kindness and joyous natural benevolence typical of Myanmar's inhabitants, almost without noticing me. Only once was I the object of an ill-tempered gesture, when I photographed a passer-by who had filled his bag with brioches taken from the altar, for his own breakfast.

The story of the altar turned out to be exceptional, well beyond the matter of impermanence that had fascinated me. It was destroyed by a mad woman who had taken up residence in one of the two adjoining shelters. The shelter was tiny – sufficient only for sleeping in a crouched position, or sitting with an arched back. The other shelter was occupied by two water containers installed to quench the thirst of passers-by, a tradition of Buddhist charity seen even in the most remote paths of Myanmar. I would never have imagined my transformation, from witness to rescuer, and that my photographic diary of cultual practices was about to reflect a dramatic turn of events. However, at first, I continued to limit myself to my role as a witness. I remained neutral when madness invaded Bobogyi's space and came to sleep nearby: when the mad woman tore off his white parasol, used its white cloth to make a shawl for herself, then, a few days later, put it back on the altar and set it on fire. I remained standing still when I discovered Bobogyi occupying his usual domain, his staff in his hand, alone in the middle of the deserted altar, emptied of everything. I felt I must remain an eyewitness, respectful of this neighborhood cult, whatever was happening to it. Even if I spoke Burmese, I was a stranger. This worship was not mine. Thus, when I saw, behind the banyan, the statuettes and the cult objects from the altar, which I had photographed for months, floating between the tall grass of the brook, I continued to shoot as usual. The pathetic situation of these holy images endowed my report with an unexpected dimension: the destruction of the Bobogyi altar by a mad woman.

At the same time, I had become accustomed, perhaps even attached, to these statuettes that would soon follow the water's current to disappear I knew not where. Why not rescue them from their watery fate? Should I confine myself to my status as a witness? Was I not locking myself into a rigid mental attitude? Was not I a human being with initiative? Was not history - life - made of these encounters, intrusions and shocks between indigens and foreigners? After all, my role could be to pick up the floating remnants and put them back where I had seen them for months, no need to dither about the water's color. But at the same time, I had contrary thoughts: was not it the fate of Golden Valley's Bobogyi altar to experience this crisis and the subsequent renewal of its ritual elements? Should I not let things happen? Was not the little brook, where the statuettes and the frames floated, symbol, or rather sign, of this will? Would my intervention not break the sacred course of things? A selfish act, this is what I dreaded most. On the other hand, maybe the mad woman had integrated me into the court of Bobogyi's devotees? Photographing her, sometimes very closely, I ended up taking a place in her litany to become "the photographer". Besides, the whole neighborhood knew me – on days when I had failed to show up, guardians of the houses near the altar invariably asked me where I had been.

Sitting on the embankment, I watched the dripping statuettes that I had just retrieved and placed on the white metal tray where so many offerings had been deposited. No one today would imagine the force of the mental drama that swept the altar, set it on fire, and cast the images to the stream. Ultimately, the strength of the love and hopes of Bobogyi's devotees restored things to their place of harmony at the little crossroads, under the glance of watchful squirrels.

At the crossroads

The sanctuary of Bobogyi in Golden Valley is flanked by two small wooden stilt shelters. In the shelter on the right are two big bottles of drinking water to quench the thirst of the passers-by – an expression of the Buddhist charity omnipresent in Burma. Traditionally, they were earthen pots that kept the water cool. In the shelter on the left are statuettes and various kinds of offerings. During the repainting of the statue of Bobogyi, this shelter was used to the cult objects. Its most exceptional use was when it served as shelter for a mad woman who slept there for several weeks before setting fire to the Bobogyi sanctuary, having assumed his identity, and then leaving the neighborhood. Since the reopening of University Avenue, where the residence of Aung San Suu Kyi is located, this small road has become a busy shortcut, especially from the Shwedagon.

The shrine of Bobogyi is surrounded by many Buddhist monasteries.

The door is never locked, only pushed shut. In this part of the altar, behind a bouquet of flowers, there is a tray with the same basic ritual offerings (coconut and bananas) as for the Buddha and *nat*. On the right, an alms bowl on the lid of which is an offering of pink flowers. On the shelf above are the Chinese monk U Ti Bwa, and the *weikza* Bo Min Aung and Bo Bo Aung. The existence and arrangement of the statuettes inside the Bobogyi shrine varies considerably according to the donations and the people who take care of it.

This street vendor regularly offers bouquets of flowers to Bobogyi (66). Most offerings are made by the inhabitants of the neighborhood and by those who come to work there – usually domestic staff: housekeepers, cooks, security guards, drivers; or directors of real estate, cosmetics, and construction agencies.

Helped by his driver, this shareholder of a *thanaka* company (a powder made from crushing the bark of the *thanaka* tree that Burmese, especially women, traditionally put on their face, and sometimes even over their whole body) makes an offering every morning, shortly after dawn, of thirty or so brioches to Bobogyi . . .which will be quickly grabbed and eaten by passers-by, but also by squirrels, crows and rats who live around the banyan and eagerly await their arrival (63).

The altar of the guardian of the banyan

The altar during the night and at dawn.

The shrine of Bobogyi is located under the banyan of which he is the guardian. In this sense, it is associated with this tree which played an important role in the life of the historical Buddha. None of the elderly neighborhood denizens remember the exact origin of Bobogyi worship at this location, but it goes back at least seventy years. Bobogyi was then represented by a wooden statuette at the foot of the banyan. The current sanctuary, which dates back about fifteen years, was funded by the devotees of the neighborhood. There is thus no owner of this sanctuary nor a person in charge of its cult. The statue of Bobogyi, purchased at the Buddhist market of the Shwedagon, was a collective purchase, like the metal structure that houses it. Nonetheless, devotees can make private donations, such as shelves. When these gifts are important, the donors names are recorded, as for example for the tiled floor.

Bobogyi is a religious figure: he is dressed in white, a color worn by some lay people who practice Buddhist asceticism, he wears the tiara of a divinity and a prayer scarf (*tabe*) placed on the ground during devotions. Finally, he holds a pilgrim's stick and a rosary. His white parasol is a royal attribute. The colored paper pennants are ritual prescriptions related to vows (*yadeya*). The copper banyan leaves around the rim of the parasol make a soothing sound and are found in almost all pagodas over Burma.

Behind Bobogyi, are several paintings under glass brought by the devotees, including those of Myinbyushin, the Lord of the White Horse, one of the *nat* of the pantheon of the Thirty-seven Lords and, on the right, that of Thuratati, guardian of the Buddhist canon. Formerly, they were objects of worship common in people's houses, before being replaced by statues.

Like the Buddha statues in orange drapes during the cool season, these woolen scarves were made to warm Bobogyi. His clothing includes, in addition to thin and light summer scarves, jackets and *longyi* (46).

There is no ritual before starting to repaint Bobogyi, the workers just need to bow down to him. The sanctuary is then emptied of its cult objects, leaving behind only the statue, whose base is sealed at the tiled base of the sanctuary. The metallic grey dress was repainted in white, and the black scarf in brown. Although these painters were initially engaged by one of the devotees to paint his house, this repainting of Bobogyi and his sanctuary was decided by mutual agreement between all the devotees.

The repainting lasted for two days. Once the paint dried, the facial features were added. The forehead wrinkles, made in the cement of the statue, have not been repainted as in the old version, but left flesh-colored. Unlike the statues of Buddhas and *nat*, there was no ritual animation: i.e. the consecration of the statue that makes it an object of worship, because the cult of Bobogyi is not an organized but a spontaneous worship.

A solar panel is used to power the lamp that illuminates the sanctuary at night. Power cuts, still frequent, and the difficulty of connecting the Bobogyi shrine to the nearby house, have resulted in this practical and inexpensive solution. Its installation was carried out by two of Bobogyi's devotees.

In a hot country like Burma, giving water to the thirsty is an essential act of Buddhist charity and explains the number of pots and water bottles along the roads and streets. For all the devotees questioned, the water in the shelter next to the shrine had particular virtues ...although they could not articulate which virtues they had in mind. They associate it with the "sphere of blessings" that define the sanctuary's boundaries. Passers-by drink a glass or more, and neighbors come to fill larger containers.

The *aung tebyé* whose name means "success" is a ritual foliage. The water of the shelter used for the offerings establishes a direct link between this water and Bobogyi.

The cult

Every day the most varied offerings are made to Bobogyi: flowers in bouquets, garlands, cut petals in a cup, incense sticks, white and red and more rarely gilded candles, oil lamps, rosaries, parasols, fermented tea leaves (55), betel quid (52), brioches, plain water in a glass, banknotes, cigarettes, scarves, jacket, and *longyi*. Alcohol is never offered, unlike the case in the sanctuaries of some *nat*. These offerings reflect the seasons (flowers, summer and winter clothes) and the constant care taken by the devotees to maintain the shrine: one throws away the faded flowers, another changes the scarves, etc. Also of note are the holy images that surround the statue of Bobogyi brought here as additional objects of devotion with no other link than the sanctity of the place. Likewise, at the foot of the banyan guarded by Bobogyi, the sacred "rejects" pile up: either old ones from the sanctuary itself, or else from the altars of the whole ward. Time, wind and rain are left to take care of what clutters the family altar and cannot be thrown away like rubbish.

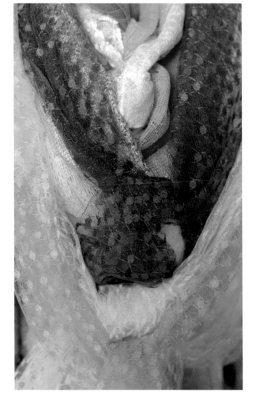

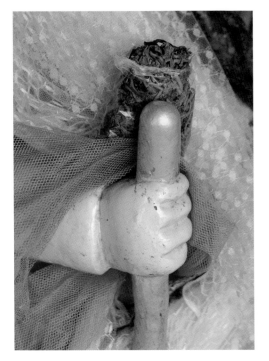

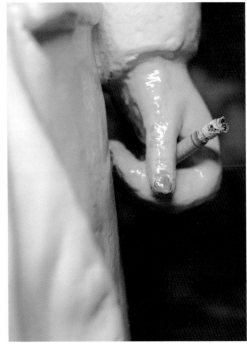

Popcorn, offered here to the Buddha, evokes the prosperity associated with puffed rice used in some
Buddhist rituals: i.e. novitiation, consecration of statues, etc. It is then thrown over the assembled crowd.
Popcorn is also given to fish and turtles in the ponds of Buddhist temples.

A very popular *nat* which does not belong to the pantheon of the Thirty-seven Lords, Pegu *medaw* the goddess
with the form of a female buffalo, is represented here by a statuette and a painting on glass.

This *naga* deity (her headdress shaped like a dragon's head) emerges from the middle of a clay bowl which symbolizes a basin. She is the spouse of Min Maha Giri, the head of the Thirty-seven Lords, and the bowl is often seen under the coconut representing him in people's houses.

U Min Kyaw: one of the Thirty-seven Lords.

Left: Thuratati between two honorary parasols, one of which will soon end up at the foot of the banyan with other cult objects (58). Right: Myinbyushin, the Lord of the White Horse.

One of the day's offerings put in the side shelter before being moved to the foot of the banyan.

Behind the shrine of Bobogyi, at the foot of the banyan, are piled up objects of worship, sometimes very recent items. The red fans edged with white are used for the ritual animation of the coconut for Min Maha Giri: the person who makes him an offering, fans him. The woven bamboo baskets served as a support for the coconut that was offered to him. Chinese decorations were brought shortly after the Chinese New Year celebration.

From left to right: paper-cut pennants, red fans, Myinbyushin white horse, a bird cage, a Buddha throne, and a small domestic altar.

The devotees

These two men at left touch the hand of Bobogyi holding the stick because it is supposed to have a healing effect. Good health is one of Bobogyi's most requested wishes. A 47-year-old woman told me that she has never taken any medicine and is still healthy since she worships him. After health, the most frequent wishes concern family happiness, work, protection against diverse dangers, and exam success. According to the devotees, their fidelity is explained by the effectiveness of Bobogyi's power: "What is wonderful is to have your wishes fulfilled ... Bobogyi is really powerful, I always get what I ask of him ... I dreamed of Bobogyi and he helped me ... If Bobogyi wants to say something he visits us in dreams. "

After their prayer and offering, the devotees ring the bell.

Street vendors, collectors of cartons, glass and metal, passers-by, drivers, but also wealthy landowners: Bobogyi is revered by all, no matter to which class of society they belong to. This Burmese lady, coming to offer white roses to Bobogyi, has a house rented to an embassy.

Bobogyi is revered by Buddhists but also by Hindus, such as this woman of Indian origin.

Early morning brioches

For years, every morning, a pious retired businessman offers thirty brioches to Bobogyi. When he cannot come, his driver, like here, carries out the donation. Every other day, two hundred brioches are delivered to him at home. He offers a first part to his domestic Buddhist altar, then goes with a small van to three places: first to the Bobogyi sanctuary, then to two other banyans of the neighboring ward, guarded by two *yokkaso*. On the way, he also distributes brioches to dogs and crows. These offerings are useful because they are consumed by people who are often poor, and by the animals associated with the sanctuary: the squirrels and crows in the branches of the banyan, the rats whose burrows plunge between its roots, and the dogs of the ward.

The flower seller

I have bought many bouquets from the flower seller, who soon became a friend, and whom I met several times a week at the Bobogyi shrine or in one of the alleys of the Golden Valley labyrinth. Arriving at the sanctuary, he always began by drinking the water and then carefully arranging the flowers he selected in vases.

It is from the flower seller that I learned to blow on the roses just before offering them, having removed the protective fishnet. By blowing very lightly on their petals, they open and the flower blooms.

The mad woman

Every day, for several months, I went before sunrise to the shrine to photograph its slightest changes.
One morning, I was surprised when I saw a body draped in a blue cloth, asleep in one of the two shelters.
The body was breathing and a little later sat up, but still without revealing its face.

What a surrealistic spectacle this ghostly form created in the presence of
two women performing their donations as if nothing had happened. One is
offering a brioche to a dog, the other lighting candles. The blue form remained
immobile for about 15 minutes before moving, its face and arm, only to
embark on an intense monologue that never stopped.

The mad woman was so invested in
her monologue that she remained
oblivious when I approached to take
a close-up shot.

She spent nearly two weeks in her shelter, only going out for a meal. Then one morning, everything disappeared: she, and all of the sanctuary's contents. Only the statue of Bobogyi was still in place. The bottles of water also had disappeared, their shelter knocked over. In the mad woman's mind, had it been necessary to clean the sanctuary and to throw everything away?

The contents of the Bobogyi shrine, the objects deposited at the foot of the banyan or hung around the trunk, and the two bottles of water . . .were thrown by her into the stream.

After a quarter of an hour of
procrastination, I retrieved the
statuettes of U Ti Bwa, Bo Bo Aung
and the Buddha, as well as the
offering tray, that I replaced in the
sanctuary together with a statuette
of Pegu *medaw* and a glass painting
of Shinbyushin. The two aluminum
shelves having been spared, I placed
U Ti Bwa and Bo Bo Aung on one
side and the Buddha on the other. I
felt the tray would encourage new
offerings and the sanctuary would
come back to life.

Having lit a fire inside the sanctuary, the mad woman rang the bell, as if her de-structuring act was an offering. A little later, the umbrella she had found somewhere ended in ashes at the foot of Bobogyi. Finally, the sanctuary was locked.

I bought a new umbrella at the Shwedagon Buddhist market, but the mad woman grabbed it soon after, turning it into a shirt for herself, and by wearing it, becoming Bobogyi.

Re-emergence of the cult

Finally, the sanctuary reopened and regained its function, allowing Bobogyi's devotees to express their wishes and gratitude.

Endnotes

1   In this paper, *bobogyi* is in italics when used as a vernacular generic term, without a plural mark. When referring to the address term or as a title, it is written as Bobogyi, starting with a block letter, as in Mandalay Bobogyi.

2   See pages 28-33.

3   This Bobogyi owes his appellation to the huge banyan (*shwe nyaung bin*) under which his cult has developed. In 1981, when I first visited his shrine, some miles to the North-West of Yangon, there was just a small wooden shrine with a wooden figurine inside. But the shrine was already visited by the new owners of cars coming to present their vehicles to have them blessed by the spirit. Shwe Nyaung Bin Bobogyi was then the only spirit specialized in the protection of cars. Since this first visit, the small wooden shed has developed in a permanent concrete shrine to accommodate the numerous cars driven there to get the *bobogyi*'s blessing. Other spirits such as the Thingangyun Bobogyi are addressed today to get cars blessed.

4   Sadan 2005, p. 90.

5   See Temple 1906, Spiro 1967, Brac de la Perrière, 1989.

6   U Min Kyaw is the Lord of Shweguni, an island near Pakhangyi, at the confluence of the Chindwin and Irrawaddy rivers, whose festival is celebrated in March by thousands of spirit mediums and their followers. U Min Lay is the youngest of the two Taungbyon brothers, settled in a village to the North of Mandalay, whose main celebration occurs in August. Alon Bobogyi is the Lord of the eponym city and is feasted after the Lord of Shweguni,

at the turn of March-April. Myinbyushin is the Lord of the White Horse.

7   Temple 1906.

8   Spiro 1967, p. 45, 46, 68.

9   See figure **48**. Bo Min Gaung is the most popular among worshipped *weikza* figures today. He "went out" in 1952 at Mt Popa were he was practicing religion according to the *weikza* path requirements since the Second World War. Since his disappearance he has become a cult object by *weikza* path followers being supposed to come to the rescue of those Buddhist fellows obeying the precepts and practising meditation. He progressively gained fame in such a way that he is now the focus of the main *weikza* yearly festival at Mount Popa, around the full moon of September (See Brac de la Perrière, 2014)

10 Sadan 2005, p. 105.

11 Ibid.

12 In 2004, the capital was moved far to the north, to Naypyidaw, a new administrative city erected from scratch in the parched central plain of Burma.

13 For the Shwedagon story as related in the Dhammaceti inscription see Pe Maung Tin 1934, Pearn 1939 and Stadtner 2011. The inscription is trilingual, running over three slabs, with one slab per language, in Pali, Mon and Burmese. The basic narrative of the historical Buddha's gift of hair relics to Tapussa and Bhallika, during his lifetime, is found in Sri Lankan commentaries from the 5th century (both Buddhaghosa and Dhammapala) but it is only in the fiveteen-century Dhammaceti stele that these hair relics are identified in

Burma with those enshrined on the site of Shwedagon, at Yangon (Pearn 1939 p. 9 and Stadtner 2011 p. 76).

14 Pe Maung Tin, 1934:33. The chronicle quoted by Pe Maung Tin is the *Lik Wan Dhat Kyaik Lagun*.

15 Pe Maung Tin, 1934:51-52. See also the Burmese history of the pagoda dated from 1924, *Shwe Dagon Thamaing Athit*.

16 See for instance Asara, 1955 and also Pearn 1939 p. 9 and Stadtner 2011 p. 84.

17 Brac de la Perrière 1995. See also here p. 5-11.

18 Stadtner 2011 p. 110.

19 Ibid.

20 Id., p.111.

21 Id.

22 Id., p. 86.

23 Thai-style glass amulets are now seen on display also in a small stand of the Sule pagoda (**25**). This newly sold religious commodity may well spread further with the development of regional tourism.

24 Nyun Wai, 1989.

25 Sadan 2005, p. 105.

26 Brac de la Perrière 2011, p.176.

27 Asara 1953. This second legend of Buddhicization refers to the king of Suvanabhumi (see p. 3, 4), the first to King Okkalapa.

Location of the Bobogyis shrines[*]

OUTSIDE YANGON

- *Mandalay Bobogyi* is at the foot of Mandalay hill in Mandalay.
- *Hmawbi Bobogyi* is in Hmawbi, as part of the Zambu Mara Aung Zedi Daw, the main pagoda. Hmawbi, is 40 km northwest of Yangon.
- *Yayle Bobogyi* is part of the Yayle *hpaya* (pagoda in Burmese), in Kyauktan, about 30 km southeast of Yangon.
- *Shwe Nyaung Bin Bobogyi* is on the left side of the road going to Bago, about 500 m. before the War cemetery. This is also the road going to Hmawbi Bobogyi.
- *Thanlyin Bobogyi* is part of the Kyaikkhauk *hpaya*, in Thanlyin, about 10 km south of Yangon. This is also the road to Kyauktan Bobogyi.
- *Thwante Bobogyi* is part of the Shwesandaw *hpaya*, in Thwante.

To go there, cross the Yangon river at the Pansodan Pier, a hundred meters from the Strand hotel, to reach Dala from where a taxi can be hired until Thwante, about 20 km from Dala.

IN YANGON

- *Botataung Bobogyi* is in Botataung *hpaya*, one of the most renowned Buddhist pagodas in Myanmar, right on the bank of the Yangon river.
- *Golden Valley's Bobogyi* is next to the New Zealand embassy, in Inya Myaing Road.
- *Kyaikkasan Bobogyi* is located near he intersection of the Yadanar and Thiri Mingalar Roads. The *former Kyaikkasan Bobogyi* is now in the Thingangyon Bobogyi shrine.
- *Shwedagon Bobogyi* is on the upper terrace of the Shwedagon *hpaya*, the most renowned Buddhist pagoda in Myanmar.
- *Sule Bobogyi* is on the terrace of the Sule *hpaya*, one of the most renowned Buddhist pagodas in Myanmar.
- *Tamway* **bobogyi** are located at the Tamway crossroads (Shwegondain, U Chit Maung and Banyardala Roads).
- *Thamaing Bobogyi* is located in the Thamain Budayon Road, close to its intersection with Insein Road.
- *Thingangyon Bobogyi* is located on the right side of the Lay Daungkan Road, a hundred meters before the Nga Moe Yeik bridge.
- *Yangon Bobogyi* is in the garden at the foot of the Shwedagon (southwest side).

---

[*] The information provided here, together with the photographs, allows to reach all the shrines mentioned in the text (see the two maps: fig. 23 a, b, and the Index).

Index

Acknowledgements

The authors are grateful to Narisa Chakrabongse and her team at River Books for having brought this manuscript to light beautifully, to Donald M. Stadtner for his useful suggestions and comments on the history and Buddhism of this study, to Lilian Handlin for having gone through the successive versions, and to Elizabeth Moore and Roy Hart for the ultimate checks. They also wish to offer their thanks to the devots and the persons in charge of the shrines of Bobogyi for their always kind collaboration.

Bénédicte BRAC DE LA PERRIÈRE Ph. D., is a CNRS senior researcher and a member of the Center for Southeast Asian Studies (CASE) in Paris. She is an anthropologist specializing on Burma where she has regularly conducted field research since the 1980's. She is the author of *Les rituels de possession en Birmanie: du culte d'Etat aux cérémonies privées* (ADPF, 1989) and has co-edited several collective volumes. Among the latest are: *Les apparences du monde. Royautés hindoues et bouddhiques de l'Asie du Sud et du Sud-Est* (with M.-L. Reiniche, EFEO, 2006), *Power, Authority and Contested Hegemony in Burmese-Myanmar Religion* (with H. Kawanami, *Asian Ethnology* 68.2, Nanzan Institute for Religion and Culture, 2009) and *Champions of Buddhism. Weikza Cults in Contemporary Burma* (with G. Rozenberg and A. Turner, NUS Press, 2014).

Cristophe MUNIER-GAILLARD is living in Myanmar since 1999 where he worked as a Burmese interpreter for the ICRC (2000-2007). In 2015, he obtained a Ph. D. from Paris IV-Sorbonne University on Burmese Buddhist narrative murals. In 2016-2017, he held a seminar on mural styles at the Department of Archaeology at the Yangon University. His main publications are *Burmese Buddhist Murals. Volume 1 – Epigraphic Corpus of the Powin Taung Caves* (with Myint Aung, 2007) and *La vie du Bouddha. Peintures murales de Haute-Birmanie* (with A. Kirichenko and Aung Kyaing, 2017). He is the editor of *Mural Art. Studies on Paintings in Asia* (River Books, 2018). As a photographer, he published *Yangon-Eden*, an essay on Yangon urban metamorphosis (Pansodan Books, 2018 and *Journal of the Burma Studies*: Northern Illinois University, 2018).

Donald M. STADTNER was for many years an Associate Professor (University of Texas, Austin), after receiving his Ph. D. in Indian art (University of California, Berkeley). His publications include *Ancient Pagan* (2005), *Sacred Sites of Burma* (2010) and *Sacred Sites of Sri Lanka* (forthcoming 2019). He also co-curated *Buddhist Art of Myanmar*, Asia Society, New York, and contributed to the catalogue (2015). He was co-author of *The Jeweled Isle: Art from Sri Lanka*, Los Angeles County Museum of Art (2018). He divides his time between the San Francisco Bay Area and research trips to India, Burma, Thailand and Sri Lanka.